VAN MADE RECIPES

a healthy cookbook for living on the road

BY EMILY MURRAY

stickyearth.com publishing

Stickyearth.com Publishing

Paperback ISBN 978-1496058546

Photography by
Emily Murray
Dave Meszaros

Printed in the United States of America

TABLE OF CONTENTS

Introduction

This book is written by a budget traveler for a budget traveler, but anyone who is sometimes lazy or frugal will also benefit from the recipes in this book. The recipes are inexpensive and healthy. They can be made on a one- or two-burner stove (or open fire) with limited sources of water. There are a lot of fresh vegetables in these recipes, so if you do not have a refrigerator I recommend buying items that perish quickly on, or the day before preparing the food.

I try to keep the recipes very simple with only a few main ingredients and basic spices. Even with simple recipes there are times while living on the road when you may get too tired, or it's too dark, or you have to be undercover and cannot make a meal to its full potential. Therefore, each recipe includes a "lazy version" which is a simpler way to eat the food you bought.

I am mostly a vegetarian so the recipes are mostly vegetarian as well.

You will only need a few supplies to make these recipes. The first is a source of heat: a camp stove, an open fire, a grill, or any other creative ways to heat your food. You will need pots and pans. I have a set of camping ones that all fit inside each other to save space. I love them and highly recommend them. Some have holes on the lids for draining water and bowls that fit inside. You will also need a cutting board and cooking and eating utensils.

So you need:
- Stove/Fire/heat
- Pots and Pans
- At least one bowl per person
- Eating and cooking utensils

Gardening on the road

Sprouts are an easy thing to grow without soil or a mess. By the nature of van life, sprouting beans is much easier than preparing beans the traditional way.

Two good beans to sprout are **Mung Beans** (these are the bean sprouts used in some Asian dishes) and Chick Peas because they are easy and quick. However there are tons of different kinds of seeds that are good for sprouting. Check with any health food store for a variety of options. The quicker sprouts only take about three days until they are ready to eat.

The benefits of eating sprouted beans seeds and grains, and all the different ways to grow them is a whole other book in itself. This is how I grow them.

You will need:

- Glass jar
- Inexpensive mesh from a fabric store
- Beans or other seeds for sprouting
- Rubber band

Sanitize your sprout jar before you use it and in between every crop. I do this by boiling the jar in water. Use caution!

After your jar has been sanitized add about a half an inch of beans to the bottom.

- Secure a square of mesh to the top of the jar with a rubber band. Make sure the sprouts always have air. Do not close off the top of the jar.
- Rinse beans well with water.
- Soak beans in water overnight.
- Drain the water in the morning and rinse the beans again.
- Keep the sprouts out of direct sunlight.
- Remove loose hulls and duds as you see them.
- Rinse the beans 2-3 times daily for a few days.
- Once tails have grown a quarter of an inch they are ready to eat.

Cook them or eat them raw. Go easy if this is the first time you are eating raw sprouts. Your digestive system may need to get used to them.

Growing herbs inside your vehicle is easy and fun, adding freshness to many of your van-made dishes.

For a cheap herb pot take an empty nut can and attach it to the counter using Velcro. This keeps it from moving around while you are driving and removable if you are parked in a nice sunny spot so you may move the plant outside. Fill the can with soil and sprinkle any herb seeds of your choice.

Remember to water daily and watch them grow.

Groceries

FARMERS MARKET FRESHNESS

The easiest food to eat sometimes can be the most nutritious and delicious. One of my favorite things to eat on the road is sliced fresh veggies with a sprinkle of salt.

If you see a farmers market on the road or at home stop by to support. Farmers markets provide some of the finest, cheapest, and freshest produce you can get your hands on. They are also a great place to meet a community you are passing through. Try samples of fruits with crazy names, new varieties of your favorite vegetables, unlabeled wines, and prepared foods.

Shake the hand of the person who grew your dinner.

Tip: When washing produce with limited sources of water give your small items a bath instead of a shower. Use a large pot and fill with water, then dunk and swirl until clean. For larger fruits clean the outside with vinegar and a paper towel.

VAN KITCHEN STAPLES

Canned beans of all sorts

Salt, pepper, your favorite spices

Canned tuna

Olive oil

Apple cider vinegar for recipes

Inexpensive white vinegar for cleaning

Food vehicles to deliver the food from plate to mouth (crackers, bread, pitas, chips)

Soy Sauce

Bouillon cubes

Noodles, rice, pasta

Dehydrated food like mushrooms or soy protein

Chopped olives

Sesame seeds

Onions

Garlic

Limes

Tomatoes

Avocados

Located in the back of the book is a recipe index. Use it if you are looking for something to make out of food you have on hand.

RECIPES

GUACAMOLE AND CHIPS

A classic snack.

Ingredients:

- 2-3 ripe avocados
- 1 tomato
- Juice of one lime
- The smallest onion you can find (like the diameter of a silver dollar)
- Salt, pepper, and cilantro to taste
- Bag of tortilla chips

Directions:

1. Mash the avocados in a small pot.
2. Cut tomato into tiny bite size chunks.
3. Slice onion into thin slices.
4. Add tomato, onion, lime juice, and spices into the mashed avocados and stir.
5. Dip chips into guacamole.

Lazy Version:

Don't feel like cleaning the guacamole bowl?

Cut Avocado into 4 quadrants (this makes the pit easy to remove)

Cut quadrants into thin slices without cutting through the skin.

Cut tomato into similarly sized slices.

Scoop avocado out of the skin with tortilla chip.

Place tomato on top and munch.

RAW VEGGIE SALAD

Don't take this list of ingredients too seriously. Put whatever you like or have on hand in it. I've done a bunch of ways and they were all delicious. This is my favorite so far!

Ingredients:

- 1 orange bell pepper
  (these are the sweetest bell peppers)
- 1 tomato
- 1 cucumber
- Fruit (recommended: strawberries or a pear)
- 1 can of chick peas − drained − and rinsed if possible
- Apple cider vinegar (or any vinegar)
- Salt to taste

Directions:

1. Chop all the vegetables into bite size pieces.
2. Put fruit and beans in bowl.
3. Sprinkle salt as desired.
4. Use enough apple cider vinegar to coat everything.
5. Mix it all up.

Lazy Version:

You can never go wrong with a cucumber, salt, and vinegar.

TOMATO BASIL MOZZARELLA

Wondering what do to with that really awesome tomato you found at a roadside fruit stand?

Ingredients:

- 2 large tomatoes
- 1 ball of mozzarella
- Handful of basil leaves
- Saltine crackers
- Olive oil
- Salt and pepper

Directions:

1. Cut tomatoes and mozzarella into thin slices.
2. Place crackers on a dish and top with tomatoes, mozzarella, and basil.
3. Drizzle olive oil on top and sprinkle on a little salt and pepper.

Lazy Version:

Eat the tomato like an apple with a bit of salt, Delicious!

BEET AND CHICKPEA MIX-UP

Ingredients:

- 1 can of julienned beets-drained
- 1 can of chick peas-drained and rinsed
- 1 small onion-chopped
- Olive oil
- Apple cider vinegar
- Soy sauce
- Salt and pepper

Directions:

1. Add cans of drained beets and chick peas into pot.
2. Coat with enough just enough olive oil and apple cider vinegar to coat everything.
3. Add a dash of soy sauce and a sprinkle of salt and pepper.
4. Mix all ingredients together.

Lazy Version:

Eat can of chickpeas with a dash of soy sauce and/or Gomasio (seaweed with sesame seeds.)

EXTRA NOODLE SOUP

Ingredients:

- 4 cups of water
- Roughly 3.5ounces or 100 grams of vermicelli noodles (the short kind)
- 2 bouillon cubes (chicken flavored)
- Pinch of parsley (optional)

Directions:

1. Bring 4 cups of water to a boil.
2. Add noodles, bouillon and parsley.
3. Return to a boil.
4. Reduce heat and simmer for 5 minutes.
5. Let cool and eat.

Lazy Version:

Use packets of premixed soup and follow instructions.

OR

Heat up can of soup.

MISO SOUP WITH SPROUTS

Ingredients:

- 4-3/4cup instant seaweed miso soup packets *(most affordable packets can be found in Asian grocery stores)*
- 100 grams udon noodles
- sprouts

Directions:

1. Bring 2 cups of water to a boil.
2. Add udon noodles.
3. Reduce heat and cook for 10 minutes.
4. Drain water and set noodles aside. (optional) Rinse noodles if possible.
5. Bring 2 fresh cups of water to a boil.
6. Turn off heat.
7. Add miso soup packets, cooked udon noodles, and sprouts.

Lazy version:

Make miso soup packet according to directions.

Add sprouts.

RICE AND BEANS AND THEN SOME

Ingredients:

- 1 cup rice
- 2 cups water
- 1 onion
- 1 tomato

- Olive oil
- Spices
- 1 can of cannellini beans or kidney beans

- Handful of dehydrated* or can of mushrooms

Directions:

1. Bring water, rice, and dehydrated mushrooms to a boil. (Leave mushrooms on top so you can remove them easily to stir fry.)

2. Reduce heat to simmer until all water is absorbed.

While rice cooks . . .

3. Cut onion and tomato into bite size pieces.

4. Fry onion in olive oil on medium high heat until brown on edges.

5. Add mushrooms and continue to cook for 2 more minutes.

6. Reduce heat to medium and add tomato and cook for 2 more minutes.

7. Add beans and whatever spices you have on hand (try: salt pepper, cumin, mint, and oregano).

8. Cook until beans are heated the whole way through.

*Available in bulk at a very affordable price in Asian grocery stores.

Lazy Version:

Just have instant rice and beans without the frills.

Step one: Obtain **Fish**

> While in **Mexico** you can purchase an entire fish directly from fisherman for less than the price of a hamburger at your favorite fast food chain.

Step two: Obtain **grill**.

Step three: Clean fish.

Step four: Rub cilantro and pepper on fish.

> Or any signature rub you may have.

Step five: Drink a beer while fish is cooking.

> Recommendations: Pacifico, Tecate, or Corona.

Step six: Squeeze lime and lemon over fish and dig in.

> No utensils required.

Tip for Clean Up: Mexican dogs love to eat the remains and they're tough enough to handle the bones, gills, and head.

Lazy Version:

Fry in pan with a bit of oil. When in Southern California **I** guarantee if you look hard enough you will be able to find **99**cent fish tacos and if you're like me they will become a staple of your diet.

PLANTAINS AND PINTO BEANS

Ingredients:

- 2 ripe plantains*
  (yellow and black skin)
- 1 can of pinto beans
- 1 small onion
- 2 Roma or small tomatoes
- Cooking oil
- Salt

Directions:

1. Remove plantain skin and discard.
2. Slice plantain into long thin slices.
3. Fry plantains on **high heat** in thin layer of oil.
4. Constantly flip them over to cook both sides.
5. When the plantains are bright yellow and a little bit burnt on both sides they are done and you can remove them from the pan.
6. Fry thinly sliced onion in oil on medium high heat until brown on the edges.
7. Add 2 thinly sliced tomatoes and cook for two more minutes on medium high heat.
8. Add drained can of Pinto Bean and reduce to medium heat.
9. Cook for one to two more minutes until beans are heated through.
10. Remove from heat and top with cooked plantains.

*These keep very well. Buy several when you find them at a reasonable price.

Lazy Version: Plantain Fries

Only make the plantains then eat them like french-fries with salt and ketchup. So delicious.

TUNA SALAD SANDWICH

Ingredients:

- 1 can of tuna
- 1 packet of honey mustard sauce (Trust me. You'll love this.)
- Gomasio (seaweed and sesame seeds)
- 1 tomato
- 1 avocado
- 1-2 bread or bread like products

Directions:

1. Drain tuna
2. Mix tuna, honey mustard, and gomasio together.
3. Slice tomato and avocado.
4. Place on or in-between bread products and enjoy.

Tip: Experiment with different flavor packets like mayonnaise or relish. Many cafes and fast food restaurants give sauce packets out for free. Grab a handful.

Lazy version:

Save yourself a clean-up. Mix tuna and mayonnaise together in the can, leave everything else out and put it on some bread.

MACARONI FANTASY

Ingredients:

- ½ pound macaroni noodles (or any pasta or rice)
- 1 yellow onion
- 1 green pepper
- 2 large tomatoes
- 1 can of mushrooms or 1 handful of dehydrated mushrooms
- 5 cloves garlic (minced)
- Handful of dehydrated soy protein or 1 can of beans
- Olive oil
- Whatever spices you have on hand (use a little bit of everything)

Directions

1. Cook noodles according to directions putting the dehydrated mushrooms and dehydrated soy protein into the water.
2. Cut onion, pepper and tomatoes into bite size pieces.
3. Fry onions and peppers in olive oil on medium-high heat until they start to brown around edges.
4. Add mushrooms (drained from can or macaroni water) fry for 2 minutes.
5. Add tomatoes and cook 5 more minutes on medium heat.
6. Add garlic and cook for 30 more seconds.
7. Turn heat off.
8. Combine drained macaroni and soy protein with other ingredients.
9. Mix in any spices you have (try: salt, pepper, parsley, oregano, cumin, and mint).

Lazy version:

Make macaroni and cheese with a can of Cheeze Whiz.

COUSCOUS INSPIRED PASTA

Sometimes it's impossible to find couscous and sometimes its expensive Here's a delicious but cheaper dish inspired by couscous.

Ingredients:

- ½ a pound Acini Di Pepe (little ball shaped pasta)
- 1 small can chopped black olives
- 1 bouillon cube
- 1 small jar marinated artichokes
- 4 cloves garlic (minced)
- 1 tomato
- Olive oil

Directions

1. Cook pasta following directions on box, add a bouillon cube to the water.
2. Cut the tomato into bite size pieces.
3. Drain any excess water off of the pasta if necessary.
4. Pour enough olive oil to coat pasta.
5. Add all other ingredients into pasta, including all the juices from the artichoke jar.

Tip: If you do not use the whole box of pasta tape it shut so it doesn't spill.

Lazy Version:

The flavored kind that comes in the box is super easy and delicious; it's not a whole lot though so I recommend using two or three boxes. Be prepared to spend bankroll.

MUNCHIE WRAPS

Ingredients:

- 1 cup Couscous
- 3 cloves diced garlic
- 1 small can drained chopped olives
- Olive oil
- 1 avocado

- 1 head lettuce (Boston Bibb works best)
- 1 cucumber
- 1 tomato
- 2 ounces sprouts

Directions

1. Combine 1 cup of water and two tablespoons of olive oil and bring to a boil.
2. Turn off heat and stir in couscous, garlic, and olives, adding more olive oil as necessary
3. Set aside to cool.
4. Cut avocado, cucumber, and tomato into slices.
5. Lay lettuce leaf on plate and place one scoop of couscous on top with sliced veggies.
6. Wrap all ingredients inside leaf

Lazy Version:

Skip the Couscous and eat a lettuce, avocado, and tomato salad. Feel free to add salt, olive oil, and vinegar as a dressing.

INTERNATIONAL BEAN SANDWICH

Ingredients:

- 1 can refried beans
- 1 bell pepper
- 1 onion
- 2 cloves garlic
- 1 tomato
- Salt and pepper
- Pita bread

Directions

1. Slice tomato, pepper, and onion into thin slices.
2. Dice garlic.
3. Sauté pepper and onions in olive oil on medium high heat until darkened around the edges.
4. Add garlic.
5. Cook for 30 seconds on medium heat.
6. Turn flame very low.
7. Add can of refried beans and stir all ingredients together.
8. Heat until beans are warm the whole way through.
9. Place beans and tomatoes on a pita and fold in half.

Lazy Version:

Heat or don't heat the refried beans and put them on a pita.

BROCCOLI AND MUSHROOMS IN GARLIC SAUCE

Ingredients:

- 32 ounces frozen broccoli or
  2 heads fresh broccoli
- 1 small bag of frozen mushrooms or
  one large can of mushrooms
- 5 cloves of garlic
- Generous soy sauce
- Sesame seeds (optional)

Directions:

1. If using fresh broccoli wash and cut into bite size pieces.
2. Place broccoli and mushrooms in large pot and pour a generous amount of soy sauce in the pot; quarter cup or more.
3. Bring soy sauce to a boil. Mushrooms and broccoli may lose water into the pot especially if frozen.
4. Cook excess water off while continuing to stir.
5. Add garlic and cook for 30-60 more seconds.
6. Sprinkle on sesame seeds.

Lazy Version:

Steam broccoli using a half an inch of water on the bottom of the pot until broccoli turns bright green. Add a dash of soy sauce and sesame seeds.

PASTA WITH DICED TOMATOES AND CANNELLINI BEANS

Ingredients:

- 1 pound angel hair pasta
- 2 cans diced tomatoes-drained
- 1 can cannellini beans-drained and rinsed
- 5 cloves diced garlic
- Olive oil
- salt

Directions:

1. Cook pasta according to directions.
2. Drain water from can of beans.
3. Rinse can of beans by filling can with water and draining again.
4. Pour generous amount of olive oil into pasta until all pasta is coated.
5. Add beans, tomatoes, and garlic and stir.
6. Sprinkle salt to taste.

Tip: Dress your pasta up: Use a jar of pesto instead of olive oil or add a fried onion in the mix.

Lazy version:

Leave the garlic out.

HOW TO EAT SALAD IN A VAN

It is hard to impossible to keep salad and salad dressing in a van but you can buy fresh bagged salad and make your own dressing. Just follow the steps below.

1. Buy bagged salad on the day you plan on eating it. Buy the kind that is chopped and washed already to save yourself the time, water, and energy required to do it yourself.

2. Any veggies you are adding into your salad clean by spraying with white vinegar, and wiping clean with a paper towel.

3. Make salad dressing. This is simple to do. Keep the salad in the bag and pour oil and vinegar on top. There is no clean up this way.

4. Either close bag and shake vigorously or stir with a fork.

Optional ingredients to add to salad dressing:

Soy sauce

Sesame or sunflower seeds

Honey

Lemon juice

STIR FRY CON HUEVOS

Ingredients

- 1 bell pepper
- 1 onion
- 3 cloves garlic
- 4 eggs
- 2 Roma tomatoes
- Olive oil
- Spices

Directions

1. Dice onions, peppers, tomatoes and garlic.
2. Fry onions and peppers in olive oil on high heat until brown on edges.
3. Add tomatoes and cook for about 2 more minutes.
4. Add garlic.
5. Crack eggs into stir fry.
6. Stir mixture until all eggs are thoroughly cooked.
7. Sprinkle whatever spices you have on hand. Try parsley, salt, and seaweed.

Lazy version:

Scramble eggs in pan and eat the pepper and tomatoes raw with a bit of salt.

CHICKS AND CUKES

Ingredients:

- 1 can of chick peas
- 1 cucumber
- Olive oil
- Apple cider vinegar
- Soy sauce
- Gomasio or sesame seeds

Directions

1. Clean, peel, and slice cucumber.
2. Drain and rinse chickpeas.
3. Place cucumbers and chickpeas into a large pot or bowl.
4. Coat with apple cider vinegar, olive oil, and a dash of soy sauce.
5. Sprinkle with gomasio or sesame seeds.
6. Stir it all together.

Lazy version:

You could just eat the cucumber like an apple.

BLACK BEANS AND ORANGE POTATOES

Ingredients:

- 1 sweet potato
- 1 can of seasoned black beans
- Soy sauce
- Olive oil

Directions:

1. Clean, peel, and slice sweet potato.
2. Drain seasoned beans, but do not rinse.
3. Fry sweet potato in olive oil until it becomes soft.
4. Add can of black beans and cook until beans are heated throughout.
5. Top with soy sauce and serve over rice.

Lazy version:

Just heat the beans.

Ingredients

- Refried beans
- Salsa
- Avocado
- Tortilla chips
- Lime (optional)

Directions

1. Heat and/or stir contents of refried beans can or pouch with lime juice if available.

2. Slice avocado into bite size pieces.

3. Layer ingredients on top of chip.

Lazy version:

If you only eat the chips and salsa out of the can, it would require almost no work, and if you maintain a steady hand throughout the entire process, no clean up either.

RADICAL RADISH

Ingredients:

- 1 bunch of radishes
- 1 onion
- 1 bell pepper
- Handful of radish sprouts
- 3 cloves garlic
- 2 Roma tomatoes
- Olive oil
- Spices (try salt, parsley, basil, seaweed)

Directions:

1. Clean and chop all veggies
2. Stir fry radishes, onions, and pepper in olive oil on medium-high heat until onions turn opaque or start to brown on sides.
3. Add garlic and tomatoes and continue to stir fry for 1-2more minutes.
4. Add whatever spices you have on hand.
5. Remove from heat.
6. Serve over rice and top with radish sprouts.

Lazy version:

Eat veggies raw as a salad. Use olive oil vinegar and salt as a dressing. (Add lemon or lime juice if available)

WRAP IT UP FRESCO

Ingredients:

- Tortilla wraps
- Queso Fresco (Mexican cheese)
- 1 can seasoned black beans
- 1 onion
- 1 bell pepper
- 1 Roma tomato
- 1 avocado
- Olive oil

Directions:

1. Slice onion, pepper, tomato, and Queso Fresco into 1/4 inch slices.
2. Slice avocado into bite size pieces.
3. Drain can of beans but do not rinse.
4. Fry pepper and onion in olive oil until brown on edges on medium high heat.
5. In a separate pan fry **Queso Fresco** in a thin layer of olive oil over medium heat until slightly brown on the outside.
6. Add drained beans and tomatoes into pepper and onion stir fry. Continue to cook until beans are warmed throughout.
7. Layer ingredients onto tortilla wrap. Sprinkling fresh avocado slices on top.

Lazy version:

Fry the Queso Fresco and warm the beans. Layer these items on tortillas for a no-veggie-chopping kind of night.

LATE NIGHT SALSA

Ingredients:

- · 1 can corn
- · 1 can black beans
- · 2-3 Roma tomatoes
- · Juice of 1 lime
- · Salt and parsley

Directions:

1. Drain cans of corn and beans. (Rinse beans if possible)
2. Dice tomatoes.
3. Mix all ingredients together including lime juice and spices.
4. Dip with chips or mix into a salad.

Lazy version:

Skip the corn, beans, salt and parsley, but what is salsa without tomatoes. Don't forget to add some zest with the lime juice.

SIMPLY AMAZING PASTA SALAD

Double this recipe and have delicious left overs for lunch the next day.

Ingredients:

- 8oz. Tricolored rotini pasta
- 4-5 small Roma tomatoes
- 1 cucumber
- 5-6 cloves of garlic
- Olive Oil
- Apple cider vinegar
- Salt, pepper, basil, parsley

Directions:

1. Cook pasta according to directions.
2. Drain pasta and let cool.
3. While pasta is cooling chop cucumber and tomato into bite size pieces.
4. Finely dice garlic.
5. Mix all ingredients into the pot and coat with olive oil apple cider vinegar and spices.

Lazy version:

Cook the pasta and dice the garlic. After draining the pasta while the pot is still hot toss with garlic and olive oil for a nice light pasta.

ANTS ON A LOG

Ingredients:

- Celery
- Peanut butter
- Chocolate covered raisins

Directions:

1. Clean celery.
2. Fill celery trough with peanut butter.
3. Place chocolate covered raisins on top.

Lazy version:

Dip celery in peanut butter jar. Eat chocolate covered raisins by the handful.

THANK YOU

I am so lucky in this life to have the love, support, guidance, and helping hands of my friends and family and people I have met along the way. Nothing would be possible without the generosity of others.

I am so thankful for all the good people in the world the people that never met us before, but were willing to help us. From the guy who passed us our surfboards up a cliff, to the people who told us "good surfing over there" "good camping this way" or "take this route it's much more beautiful than the highway" to the angel who drove 100km and back to the nearest town to get a part for our broken down van and fixed it. Thank you all, without you none of this would have been possible, you didn't have to stop and help, you could of just kept going and your life would not have been any different, but you all did stop and help and give directions and offer advice and you helped our dream come true and I am so grateful.

And I am so grateful for the friends we met along the way. The people who came into our lives and shared good times with, uncontrollable laughter, and deep conversations, the friends that helped us time after time and and let us help them. The friends that grew together with us and became stronger with us. From the friends who let Dave and I stay in their homes and be part of their lives in Nova Scotia, to the girls at HC who were ready to have a good laugh or offer sage advice at any moment. And for the friends that are helping us turn the page to the next part of life right now, their giving seems to be unending. Thank you so much friends, for all the warmth you have created in our lives and all the beautiful things you will continue to do throughout your lives, you amazing people, thank you.

And thank you to our families, whom with love is unconditional. I hardly have the words to say how grateful we are for them. Our families are who we are, they take every step we take with us. We are woven together and this makes us strong. They fed us and provided us with warmth and shelter and encouragement our entire lives. They nursed us when we were sick and played with us when we were healthy. They are the people who made us with everything that is us, they were the first to show us through their unwavering love how to have strength, courage, love, light, and faith in this good earth. They have always supported us in every way possible and helped us in ways no one else can. We love you much words can only begin to explain it. Thank you for being there for us always and forever. We are so so grateful for you, our wonderful families.

And I am so grateful to have someone to share everything this world has to offer with, the joy, the pain, the beauty and the suffering of it. That there is someone to turn to and say "did you see that?" I am grateful that I have someone that I am happy to just to be with. Someone who will hold my hand as we journey through life together happy and free. We know we will follow each other to end of the earth because we already have. To my partner, to my other half, Dave, I love you and thank you for loving me.

When I think about all the wonderful people who have touched my life in so many different ways I am overcome with joy.

To all of you who have brought me joy

Follow @vanmaderecipes on Instagram
for updates on new recipes and tips.

For other travel and van life photos follow
@emilyrmurray and @habitualrituals.

www.vanmaderecipes.com

ABOUT THE AUTHOR

Emily Murray has been living on the road for years. Inspired by Jack Kerouac and the Beatnik writers of the 50s, at age 16 she began dreaming of hitting the road and living free. By the age of 20 she was taking 2 hour drives from her parents' home to the New Jersey and Delaware beaches for overnight camping trips with her tent, her surfboard, and her boyfriend every chance she got. Sometimes more than once a week, if the surf was good.

Eventually she started traveling for longer times and farther distances. Up and down the east coast, across the country and into other nations. When Emily was 22 her Dad bought her a Van and a new lifestyle began emerging for Emily, living on the road long term.

Throughout the next few years her boyfriend and herself built the van to be a home away from home with all the necessities and a few comforts for van life. Around the same time Emily was preparing her van she became a vegetarian.

She soon learned many ways to make her new diet and emerging lifestyle work together. With a passion for healthy food and armed with a good camera phone she began documenting the recipes she was creating in her van and put them into a book to share with fellow travelers.

Currently Emily has been traveling for 10 months long-term from Philadelphia across America through the national parks to the West Coast of North America into Mexico with no end in sight.

INGREDIENT INDEX

Made in the USA
San Bernardino, CA
06 December 2017